Self-Discipline Made Easy

A Complete Beginners Guide To Build Momentum To Succeed, Discipline The Mind Body And Spirit. Learn To How To Harness Your Will-Power, And Increase Your Mental Strength

Written By

James Foster

© Copyright 2021 - All rights reserved.

The content contained within this book may not be reproduced, duplicated or transmitted without direct written permission from the author or the publisher.

Under no circumstances will any blame or legal responsibility be held against the publisher, or author, for any damages, reparation, or monetary loss due to the information contained within this book. Either directly or indirectly.

Legal Notice:

This book is copyright protected. This book is only for personal use. You cannot amend, distribute, sell, use, quote or paraphrase any part, or the content within this book, without the consent of the author or publisher.

Disclaimer Notice:

Please note the information contained within this document is for educational and entertainment purposes only. All effort has been executed to present accurate, up to date, and reliable, complete information. No warranties of any kind are declared or implied. Readers acknowledge that the author is not engaging in the rendering of legal, financial, medical or professional advice. The content within this book has been derived from various sources. Please consult a licensed professional before attempting any techniques outlined in this book.

By reading this document, the reader agrees that under no circumstances is the author responsible for any losses, direct or indirect, which are incurred as a result of the use of information contained within this document, including, but not limited to, — errors, omissions, or inaccuracies.

Table of Contents

INTRODUCTION 7

NEGATIVE INFLUENCES 9

STEPS TO STOP OVERTHINKING 15

A GOOD NIGHT'S SLEEP 19

POWERFUL WAYS TO DEVELOP YOUR MENTAL TOUGHNESS: 41

MENTAL TOUGHNESS IN EDUCATION 47

MENTAL TOUGHNESS IN SPORT 53

CHARACTERISTICS OF MENTAL TOUGHNESS 57

SELF DISCIPLINE AND MENTAL TOUGHNESS 61

RESILIENT LEADERSHIP 79

BUILDING A RESILIENT ORGANIZATION 83

MENTAL TOUGHNESS IN BUSINESS 85

CONCLUSION 91

INTRODUCTION

Thank you for purchasing this book!

Forming good habits such as meditation, mindfulness, meaningful relationships, and adequate sleep will bring you to a position where the negative habits that contribute to overthinking will fall away. From unhealthy relationships to a cluttered living space, eliminating the things that keep you off will give way to a whole new you, prepared to face the challenges of life with a mind full of positive thoughts and concrete goals. It is my hope that you will come to know your full potential by working every day to develop better habits without feeling like overthinking cannot be removed from our life. You may retake control!

There are lots of books on the market on this topic, thank you again for choosing this one! Every effort has been made to ensure that it is as full of useful detail as possible, please enjoy!

As an adult, you may still suffer from an incomprehension about your vulnerability. Our fast-paced and violent modern industrialized environment is having an adverse effect on HSPs. You will quickly become drained, endlessly over-stimulated by everything from political abuse to the cacophony of noisy urban noises. As HSPs are a population minority, you may internalize the mores of our non-HSP society. Sadly, your physical, mental, and moral wellbeing fails as you try to fit into an over-stimulating, out-of-control environment.

If you're informed you're too emotional, a practiced rebuttal is a good thing to have open. You may say the non-HSP, "HSPs are believed to be present in about 20 percent of the population (divided equally between male and female), according to studies by Dr. Elaine Aron. The group has a more fine-tuned central nervous system, therefore we are more responsive to both positive and negative environmental stimuli. Noise, smell, bright lights, elegance, time pressure, or discomfort could be the triggers. They strive more intensely to perceive the visual input than most men. It can be a fun and difficult characteristic to have. "One note of caution is that when asking others about your sensitivity, it's necessary to use your bigotry. If you think the other individual will mock your vulnerability or underestimate it is best not to share the information. I've had some HSP students tell me their families or friends ignore their awareness statements and make them feel worse.

If you live in a majority non-HSP community, learning the art of consensus is crucial, and not expecting people to always make major changes to the lifestyle to fit you. One HSP mentioned that she had some neighbors playing their music loudly every night in her urban apartment building. She assured me she reached a deal with them to keep the music quiet during the week but they could play music louder only at certain hours on Friday and Saturday nights.

Enjoy your reading!

NEGATIVE INFLUENCES

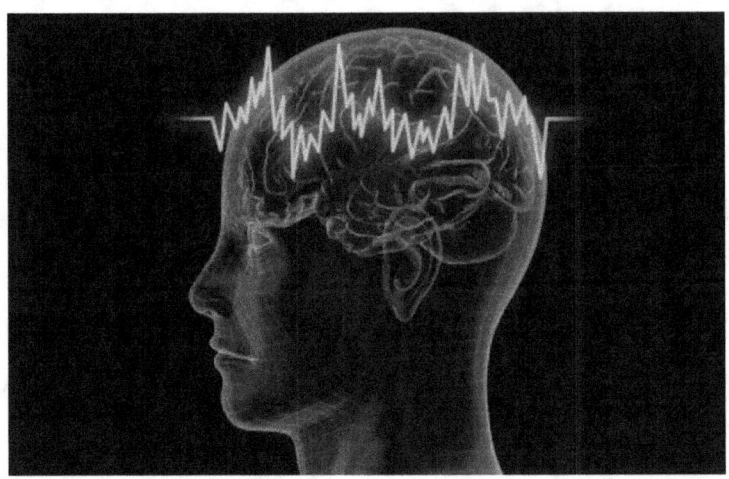

Now that we've gotten through certain tougher topics, let's talk about some other possible negative influences in your life that may still need to be addressed.

In the chapter on decent habits, we talked briefly about healthy eating. Bad eating habits are some of the toughest habits to break because they are so instantly gratifying. The same applies to habits such as drugs and alcohol which give immediate sensations of inhibition and euphoria. Don't let the shame come into play when you evaluate your eating habits. Everybody tries to eat healthily, and it doesn't make you a bad or weak person because you can't seem to stop eating the chocolate bar from the snack machine at work every day. It is a great place to start because you know it as a bad habit.

Here it is once more— take baby steps. Do not agree from now on, after having to eat chocolate every day for the past two years that you will never ever taste chocolate. I tell you... it won't happen.

Instead, limit your intake of chocolate by 1 day a week. That's Okay. If you are literally eating a Twix bar or something every single day, pick one day out of the week and set a target that day not to eat chocolate.

Getting started making healthy improvements to your eating habits is as easy as that. Though this chapter is all about completely removing negative influences, we still have to consider that changing attitudes and eradicating bad habits is not something that happens naturally.

When you buy your chocolate every day at the same location, then there are additional steps that you can take to help you get rid of that habit. Find a different route to your office, even if it's longer, that doesn't go through that vending machine, snack counter, or work cafeteria. Naturally, this will be adjusted to suit your environment, but just seeing a place that provides chocolate is a bad influence on your actions because seeing that place causes the need for the chocolate to be consumed in your brain.

The same is true in advertising. When you see those pictures of juicy hamburgers in Television commercials, it's not just because they're wanting to show their products — they subconsciously influence your cravings and put a connection in your brain that associates being hungry and craving for hamburgers every time you see this TV commercial.

Try to limit your access to those advertisements to eliminate this negative influence. As these advertisements are everywhere it can be challenging. But I'm sure you can find ways with a little imagination to remove a lot of this effect from your daily routine.

As we have discussed before, a lot of negative impacts come from the media and the images that we see there that affect us mentally like we equate positive things with the ads that we are bombarded with every day. Removing as much of that influence as possible will do much to enhance your self-esteem and positivity. And once again, it takes only one small change at a time.

In the grocery store, for example, instead of looking at the magazines and perfect bodies on the front covers, challenge yourself to listen to the voices around you, perhaps strike up a conversation with someone else in line as we have discussed before. This will remove the motif of seeing an image, and judge yourself immediately compared to what you see.

On your mobile phone and other portable devices, the same effects do occur. It may be harder to avoid such advertisements, but a good first step would be to go through your social media feeds and stop following celebrities that promote exercises or health items, and then flag advertising that will continue to appear in your feed that you no longer want to see. And the best way to eliminate this negative influence from your life would, of course, be to reduce the amount of time you spend on your mobile phone in general. Replace the hours you normally spend on the internet with something more mentally healthy to incorporate into your life, like something from your current list of interests and healthy habits. It may be challenging at first because breaking off any bad habit is always, but you'll immediately begin to see and feel the positive difference in clearing your mind from those causes.

At first, another negative influence can be hard to identify, because they view themselves as positive and vital to self-improvement. If you are inclined to listen to someone else in your life and seek advice from them, it may be time to try to break the reliance in favor of becoming more confident in your process of thinking and developing habits. Nobody knows you better than you do, as I said before, and just because something works well for someone else doesn't mean it will work perfectly for you, too. So stop watching Dr. Phil, and get your newspaper out. Hear your voice and your body. Now that you have done so much to explain your journey toward a better you, it should be much simpler. Also, be proud that you did all the heavy lifting yourself!

Changing your employment or career situation

Nothing can be more subtle in the realm of negative influence than the slow, incremental death of working a dead-end job. If you graduated from high school or college with good ideas and plans for your life, just to see them disappear as you settled down in a company you don't even care about for that boring but reliable job, it can suck you dry of all determination, passion, and energy.

If you are, be rest assured you are not alone. Our society today motivates those figures who are willing to work on the ground for a nice paycheck and even praises them. From a young age, we're inundated with the message that success is equal to money and responsibility. But the more you benefit, the more you clutter your mind and home, and the more tension you put into your life, as we've already reflected on.

Life isn't really about gain. As we discussed minimalism in the previous section, fulfillment in life does not come from valuables or moving forward in your career. If the career isn't something that you love or are passionate about, it isn't worth the commitment of your entire life. To that end, life is far too short.

This could be the last and greatest barrier that lies between you and your future self. As we are close to the end of this book and your new affirmation as a renewed human being with a clear mind prepared to be filled with positive influence and knowledge, make sure the one place you will spend most of your time all through the year is where you really want to be. Do not do this or do it because other people are telling you that it is the right thing to do. Do it, because it is where you wish to be.

STEPS TO STOP OVERTHINKING

A lot has been discussed on overthinking in this book, below are the few steps to take to stop overthinking:

1. Try to focus on the positive things that are happening right now

We have become a society that allows the prevalence of overthinking and negative thinking. You will start retraining your mind to think more positively by simply shifting your attention to what makes you happy, or to what you are grateful for. Remember: Building a house takes only one brick at a time... So you'll start to feel more fulfilled and stop overthinking, as you're not putting so much emphasis on the negativity you perceive within yourself and elsewhere

2. Say peaceful words to yourself all day.

At this particular moment, pay attention to your mind... Which kinds of thoughts are you observing? More likely, you'll find that most of your overthinking revolves around what you've got to do today, or what someone has said to make you angry, or even undermining yourself. Don't feel so bad; it's not always easy to have a consistently positive attitude with so much negative energy around us. You can combat the negative, stress-inducing thoughts with clear, peaceful words.

3. Do meditate daily.

In this book, we recommend a whole lot of meditation but for a valid reason. You stop the flow of emotions bombarding your brain every second while you meditate, and instead move into a room where silence prevails. While you don't have to turn off your brain for meditation, many people feel their minds are slowing tremendously, and with guided breaths and closed eyes, they can examine themselves much more easily.

Meditation simply brings consciousness into the body and makes everyday struggles much easier to cope with.

4. Live in the here and now.

Forget to overthink the errands you'll have to run after work tomorrow, or the bills you'll have to pay next week, or the fear of your future that you haven't even gotten up to. When you let ruminate thoughts like these, it can cause great discomfort within the body, and even lead to anxiety, depression, chronic stress, and other serious issues. Often anxiety is triggered by simply living in a time that is different from the one we have right now, so get yourself back to the present anytime you find your thoughts taking you somewhere.

5. Get out there in Nature.

Nature is the perfect way of relaxing a busy mind. You could do that in a nearby park on a weekend or during your lunch break. If you are really stressed out, think about going on a romantic holiday somewhere. Anything you can do to strengthen your relationship with nature will support your mind tremendously, and help you realize that we generate the most tension we experience in our mind and body. We lived in a position of perfect peace, and it's just a very common illusion that we see most around us. Don't get too carried away in the material world's trivial matters, because you won't find joy in numbers or things.

A GOOD NIGHT'S SLEEP

Generally what time do you go to sleep at night? This will be another task you will need to write down and keep track of for a couple of days. I think it's always more convincing to have people explain for themselves how beneficial these tips can be when advocating for better life habits. Sleep is one of the simplest aspects of our lives to overlook when focussing on self-improvement.

When we're young and in school, when you heard about the value of sleep and how much to get, there might have been a day or two in a health class. Did you say that everybody needs 8 hours of sleep to function correctly every night? Perhaps. That was always the number I had been familiar with. When you ask strangers on the street how much sleep they think they should get, odds are their answers will mostly be "8 hours." But do most of us sleep a full 8 hours each night? I know I'm having trouble getting so much, and I'm going to guess you're doing the same.

One of the most disturbing consequences of overthinking in the lives of most individuals is the fact that the worries don't cease when they lay down to go to sleep. Many of us suffering from overthinking or feeling overwhelmed with work stress, babies, family commitments, etc., will lay awake at night for hours to analyze or plan events from the previous day or the day after. We're fascinated with things we've done or said or witnessed, and we're reviewing them over and over again, wondering if we've done everything right. That's normal, and you shouldn't feel like it's something you can't fix or improve because you absolutely can.

The entire content in this book cultivates patterns that not only influence the daytime thinking processes. These will also help a lot in calming and in preparing your mind and body for sleep. You may already have witnessed this positive difference in your life, and I'm so happy for you if you have! Most people spend most of their lives having suboptimal sleep, and this again stems from cultural norms and the way society values the hard-working person.

A brave man's work is actually considered by many to work 50 hours a week. Maybe this individual has plenty of money to buy a big house, a big car, and the most comfortable bed on the market. But if he or she works that much, there's no way the individual gets 8 hours of restful nightly sleep. And for many reasons, that is harmful to a person's long-term health.

Effects of insufficient sleep

We talked earlier about the danger that you take when you deal with information overload from day to day, and how it impacts decision making. Inadequate sleep is a great example of how if you don't feed it the body can turn on you and let it rest and refill the way it was meant to. When we don't get sufficient sleep, we're depriving our bodies of vital recharge and refill time that's vital to how our brains work every day. Studies suggest driving while deprived of enough sleep is just as risky as driving while drunk. After an unrestful night, your reaction time and alertness are much lower, and just as a person who has been drinking much alcohol might think they're fine to drive, someone who just doesn't sleep well might consider it an unavoidable, normal expectation that they'll continue driving to work half asleep every morning. This is a very toxic combination of processes of thought which can have instant and life-altering effects.

But let's think of the consequences from a longer-term perspective, and less obvious. College students and working adults are known for coming in each morning and giving complaints about how they've been up all night reading or working on that big project they've got to present at weekend. People generally laugh or sympathize in response, saying they either did not sleep well, usually because they stay up late to work or read too. That's so pervasive, it seems to be an intrinsic part of American everyday life. The idea is that when you actually graduate or pull off that presentation you are praised and that losing any sleep was worth it. Okay, this may be true if it's just a night or two, but the fact is, most adults in America usually don't get enough sleep and it affects their ability to perform reliable, consistent work overtime.

Over the past couple of decades, working hours have been getting longer and longer and individuals no longer think about working 50 or 60 hours a week or working shifts going through the night. The truth is that when we don't get adequate sleep, our mental sharpness will reduce over time and we will perform worse than ever before.

Even though the effect is gradual and slow, we often do not even realize it until it is too late or we begin to make mistakes. Remember Jessica and her multitasking skills which are superhuman? Okay, just as she was so sure that she worked at an optimal level, we tend to think of operating on little or no sleep like nothing. Only when things go wrong to do we pause to consider the fact that with a low level of energy we really do feel weak and unhealthy. This sometimes comes to light only once we make these changes and commit to setting aside time for proper sleep. The difference here is day and night!

Circadian rhythm

There have been several apps released in recent years that function as tools for observing and keeping a close eye on your circadian rhythm. What is circadian rhythm, then?

Every day the body follows a natural cycle containing a plethora of chemicals and processes. The one we are going to look at is the period that follows a pattern of 24 hours, and after which we have modeled our 24-hour day. Throughout the day the body produces hormones and signals to tell our minds and bodies what they need. The biological clocks tell us when it is time to sleep and when it is time to get up. By secreting a chemical called melatonin to help calm down and prepare our bodies and minds for sleep, the body helps this cycle along. It's easy to stick to a normal and safe schedule of sleeping, waking, and eating if we obey the circadian rhythm the way we were designed. But when this routine is out of whack, we feel the effects both instantly as well as overtime depending on how long we neglect our bodies ' normal rhythms.

So, what's this natural rhythm? Is there a pattern that we should be following? Okay, like most of the decent habits that we should follow, there will be variations in the bodies of people, but when it comes to circadian rhythm, there are simple changes that you can make to see massive improvements in the way your brain works and how you feel every day.

Melatonin secretion ceases every morning, about 7:30 a.m. Your highest level of alertness happens right about 10 in the morning, according to the study. This is something I feel very strongly personally as I have always hit my peak of success and profitability between 9 and noon every day.

Ideally, if you got up sometime around 8 in the morning, you should be ready before noon for a healthy breakfast. Most adults are not allowed to decide when they eat lunch precisely if they have to adhere to a strict schedule of work. Children, on the other hand, actually follow this pattern very closely as schools typically start sometime around 8:30 or 9 and then a lunch break around noon every day. The key ingredient here is that you actually eat something that will fuel the body for the rest of the day. Eating a meal that is high in calories and low in nutrients will only lead to a large slow crash, often destroying your productivity for several hours. We will see this process happening in children as they eat a sugar reward right at lunchtime. They tend to experience a high sugar or "rush," then crash and burn soon afterward, often taking long naps or just complaining about having to do anything for the rest of the day.

According to the study, the highest level of agility and cardiovascular stamina happens in the late afternoon / early evening, and then the body starts to secrete melatonin about 11 pm, signaling that the body is ready to get some rest.

What happens during our sleep?

Most people don't realize just how effective they are at controlling and repairing their bodies. All it takes is your body to listen. With your new techniques of mindfulness and good behaviors taking over your life, listening to what your brain is telling you throughout the day should be a bit easier for you. When we listen to ad campaigns and ads trying to sell us things, we begin to notice a trend of saying that with different vitamins and other items we need to change or help the body do its work. Most of the time, this is just not true. If we put the effort into listening and making subtle changes to our daily routines, we will see and feel the difference as our bodies reward us with more strength and resilience.

So, what happens when we're actually sleeping? Sleep is a moment of significance to the body. As we sleep, the brain gets rid of the waste and recharges the structures of our body so that they are able to take on a whole new day. The cells inside our bodies are being replaced and new ones are being developed, so learning and memory is also a significant time. Have you ever been advised to "sleep on it" after having to face a difficult decision, or perhaps a challenging school lesson? That's because, when unconscious, the mind does a lot of learning, trying to integrate what we've learned, and inundating the brain throughout the day. This is the place where our minds solidify memories. Skills are fine-tuned as we learn to make their implementations better, but there's a lot of how this is embedded in our minds when we sleep. This phenomenon may have been encountered as a child when you were getting lessons or courses for a particular skill.

Maybe during your piano class, you learned a complicated set of chords and struggled to figure out exactly everything you'd learned but found that the chords came to you a little better the next morning when you sat down to play. This is part of the things the brain does for us when we are asleep and why it is so vital for us, particularly when we are young, to get an adequate amount of good sleep.

Making changes

It can be harder to change your daily habits to fit in more sleep than it seems at first. But just like any positive change in daily behaviors, you need to think about overcoming this obstacle step by step. Write a few days in your diary to watch your own sleep patterns. When do you go to bed?

Is every single night at a different time? How do you feel when you wake from your sleep? Do you have difficulty falling asleep or are you going to sleep as soon as the pillow reaches your head? Are you someone who lies awake, unable to sleep with a mind in overdrive? There are a lot of things you can do to change your nightlife habits, and prepare your body to get ready for sleep, depending on your situation.

One thing you can do is stop having late-night meals. When the body finds it hard to digest food, the signal that it's time to relax and sleep is difficult to send out. It's a bad habit for many People to eat late at night, but avoiding those late-night treats will make a big difference in how tired you feel when going to bed is time. Try to cut down on the overall amount of food you consume during the evening, and then focus on moving the time you eat to earlier in the day. Try to eat before 6 or 7 pm to allow the food to digest. This will show the body ready to start relaxing and feel the melatonin effect!

Love reading in bed? What about a half-hour search over Facebook? Well, when we do things that aren't usually associated with sleeping in the position we are meant to be resting, our brains equate bed with waking activities, making it harder to fall asleep.

Consider moving those things to a different location and reserve your bed for sleep. At first, breaking this habit may be hard, particularly if you've had the habit for so many years, but making such a transformation will go a long way towards calming your body and feeling relaxed, which is essential to fall asleep. Breaking the habit will also help reduce the urge to wake up in the middle of the night or in the morning too early, unable to fall asleep. Nothing is more frustrating than waking up an hour before the alarm should go off. Cultivate these improvements in your daily life, and you'll see a shift in sleep patterns overall.

Ultimately, my hope is that through the ideas and techniques discussed in this book you have already tackled your overthinking, but if not, it's a perfect time to start practicing meditation, or that "time out for you" strategy is right before bed. If you've spent the last hour before bed worrying about work or trying to finish those last items on your to-do list, your brain would find it much harder to wind down and prepare for sleep.

Make time early in the day for these activities, and reserve the hour before bed for relaxing.

You will begin to see significant improvements in how much strength you have in the morning, your mood, efficiency and overall sense of well-being as you continue practicing good habit-forming in relation to getting enough night's sleep. When you live with people who also have inadequate sleeping habits, consider sitting down and sharing your plans to develop fresh, safe sleeping habits with them. You will be praised by your loved ones as they too enjoy the benefits of giving the body what it needs every day.

All of the previous tips to succeed on the road to understanding will help with getting a good night's sleep to realize your dream for a new and improved you, ready to take on the challenges of life!

Winners Mindset

A performer's attitude which they will consistently win or at least deliver at their maximum level. They have strong and unwavering confidence in themselves and their professional aptitude and cumulative experience.

Hyperfocus

The ability to execute in all circumstances at a high level of performance without getting distracted and with complete mental consistency and ease. Many people call it 'in the region.'

Stress management

The ability to manage stress and pressure at the moment a job is done, fear, or anxiety without a doubt. Or at least without being dissuaded by fear and anxiety, and working independently. A master of stress optimization knows how to focus and perform better using an extremely stressful environment.

Failing well

Capable of contextualizing positively an inability to produce the results a performer intends to achieve. And to extract value and learn from the failure to perform, funnel it into the next performance to continue rising to the next level.

Maxing out limits

In the experience of pain, mental and physical stress, and physical discomfort, the ability to extract maximum physical effort and perform in spite of unpleasant sensory by-products. That could include mental compulsion, physical pain, or exertion.

Preparation

This is a planning distinction allowing the performer to be prepared for any eventuality in the performance (or before the performance) and to have a backup plan for any predictable or otherwise unforeseeable circumstance. This allows the performer to be ready for any turn of events and to remain comfortable and execute whatever the situation. This allows the performer to be prepared for any questions corner of activity and to stay healthy and perform whatever the situation. This also allows the performer to have a plan in case they succumb to a performance shortfall, and to fully recover to complete the task at hand without dialing back performance as a consequence due to deception or perceived failure or loss. And most importantly, before external validation declares a fault or damage.

Who should build or develop mental toughness?

Mental toughness skills should be learned and refined by anyone who is out to manufacture high-level results, particularly in performance-based environments such as business, competitive sports, entertainment, and high-stress jobs.

COMPANY, PROFESSIONALS, SALES TEAMS, AND ENTREPRENEURS:

Sales staff and business executives will benefit immensely from handling negative emotions and developing performance-enhancing mental toughness skills to manage companies, engaging with consumers, and marketing to customers.

ATHLETES:

Mental toughness has been developed for athletes and today elite athletes and increasingly more junior athletes use it extensively to give them an edge in competition. Mastery in mental toughness can benefit figure skaters, gymnasts, triathletes, runners, CrossFit competitors, and anyone who considers themselves (or wants to become) a high-performing athlete.

SOLDIERS and MILITARY PERSONNEL:

Staying mentally focused and undistracted may be a matter of life and death for military personnel and fighting soldiers from any branch of the armed forces – including the Army, Navy, Air Force, Coast Guard, and National Guard. Some professionals are regularly using mental toughness to carry out the tasks and perform well in their jobs.

ENTREPRENEURS:

Entrepreneurs can experience extreme hardship and challenges as they build businesses from scratch, and therefore mental toughness abilities can be critical to their success.

PERFORMING ARTISTS:

Stage, film and television performers, including musicians, actors, dancers, and other creative talents, can develop an edge over a highly competitive field by using the distinctions of mental toughness in their art. Mental toughness skills let them audition with great focus and calmness; belief in themselves; recover when they fail; perform in the zone when needed; prepare for any eventuality, and continue to deliver the success that they feel they should.

EMERGENCY RESPONDERS:

Police officers, firefighters, and paramedics, as well as other first responders, benefit immensely from mental toughness training given that their professions can put them in situations of life and death and force them into very stressful environments. Mental toughness skills can help those workers perform the jobs at a high-performance level and produce miraculous results.

MEDICAL WORKERS:

Any medical worker who is exposed to stressful environments where life and death are at stake, including doctors, nurses, and other medical staff – including operating room staff, emergency room staff, and beyond – can benefit significantly from mental toughness training to help them achieve extremely efficient, high-level results that benefit them and others.

STRESS-PRONE WORKERS:

Any worker who is exposed to stressful environments, including physicians, nurses, air traffic controllers, security personnel, and others. If you are dealing with stress and have to perform anyway, then mental toughness will give you the skills you need to do to deliver what you need.

PARENTS:

It is not accessible to the parent of children of any age and can put mothers and fathers under enormous stress and leads them to doubt their choices in raising children. Mental toughness skills can be used by ANYONE, and they are ideal for parents who not only want to pass on the training to their children to make them more resilient as they grow up but also to address the pressures, challenges, and stresses they face.

History of Mental toughness

Mental toughness is central to the study of the psychology of performance; it was initially used to help elite athletes perform better. It emerged as a study area in the mid-1980s, and research continues to this day, developing mental toughness techniques and tactics to train athletes, business people, and all performers to deliver breakthrough outcomes.

Importance of Mental toughness

Mental toughness describes the mindset that each person adopts in everything they do, and at two levels, it is critically important and valuable to everyone.

First, it explains why people and organizations are acting the way they are doing. Personality can be described as the characteristic pattern of thinking, feeling, and functioning of an individual and his personality can explain individual differences and how people act in specific situations.

Mental toughness is a character trait of personality that describes mentality. It examines what is in the individual's mind to explain why they are behaving the way they are doing. So there is an apparent connection between mentality and behavior.

One can describe mentality as both the precursor to behavior and the explanation of a lot of behavior.

Second, research and case studies from around the world show that mental toughness is a significant factor in most individuals and organizations' essential outcomes:

- Performance – explaining up to 25 percent of individual performance variation.

Mentally hard people deliver more, they work more purposefully, they show more commitment to purpose, and they are more competitive. This translates into better output, on-time delivery, and target delivery and better attendance.

- Well-being — more satisfied.

Mentally hard people show better stress management, better attendance, less likely to develop mental health problems, better sleep, and less likely to bully. They will be able to take stress in their step.

- Positive behavior - more dedicated.

Mental Tough people are more positive, have more "can do," respond positively to change and adversity, exhibit better attendance, contribute more likely to a positive culture, accept responsibility, and volunteer for new opportunities and activities.

- Learning openness - more aspirational.

Mentally tough people are more ambitious and willing to take on more risk.

Being mentally tough brings a range of benefits to individuals and organizations. Research has been conducted worldwide and has concluded that those with higher levels of mental toughness enjoy the following;

a. Better performance – it accounts for up to 25 percent of workplace performance variation.

b. Improved Positivity – more adoption of a "can do" approach that leads to more excellent relationships and connectivity with colleagues.

c. Greater well-being — more satisfaction and better stress management.

d. Change management – a calmer response to organizational change and lower stress.

e. Increased aspirations – greater ambition and trust in achieving goals and a greater willingness to persevere in doing so.

It is immensely important for these reasons to be mentally hard for an individual or an organization, especially in times of significant change. Leaders, aspiring leaders, and those working in stressful, unforgiving occupations or situations of uncertainty or dynamic change must be psychologically tough.

Organizations in the education, health, community, industry, or public sectors need to be emotionally resilient and ready for change.

POWERFUL WAYS TO DEVELOP YOUR MENTAL TOUGHNESS:

Intelligence is helpful if you want to be effective, but determination and mental toughness are mandatory. Keep track of these critical customs.

To develop and maintain the kind of mental toughness that success requires, keeping your thoughts and self-talking positive and avoiding the habits that lead to negativity and unhealthy behaviors are crucial.

The most energetic people are not those who show strength before us, but those who win battles we never see fighting against them.

Help keep yourself prepared by practicing good habits of mind and attitude for whatever comes your way tomorrow:

1.   Stable thought:

Leadership often requires you, under pressure, to make good decisions. It is important that you keep your ability to stay objective and deliver the same level of performance, no matter what you feel.

2.   Prospect:

When the world seems to have turned against you, mental strength lets you carry on. Learn how to keep your troubles in a correct perspective without losing sight of what you need to achieve.

3.   Ready for change:

If change is truly the only constant, then the most important traits you can develop are flexibility and adaptability.

4.   Underground:

If you can remember that it is not about you, you can get through setbacks and come out even more. Don't take things personally, or spend time asking Why me? Instead, concentrate on what you can control.

5. Stress-strength:

Maintain resilience to negative pressures by building your ability to cope with stressful situations.

6. Ready to challenge:

Life and business are filled with demands from everyday life, the occasional crisis, and unexpected twists. Make sure you have the resources to cope with the professional and personal crises you'll face sooner or later.

7. Concentrate:

Keep the long-term outcomes in mind to stay steady in the face of real or potential obstacles.

8. The proper attitude to setbacks:

Complications, unintended side effects, and total failures are all part of the landscape. Mitigate the damage, learn, and move on with the lessons that will help you in the future.

9. Autovalidation:

Don't worry about pleasing others: for anyone but the worst kind of waffler, that's a hit-or-miss proposition. Instead, make a focused effort to do what is right and know what you're standing for.

10. Have patience:

Don't expect results to come to fruition immediately, or rush things ahead of time. Anything that is worthwhile requires hard work and stamina; see everything as a work in progress.

11. Check:

Avoid bestowing your power on others. You control your actions and your emotions; your strength lies in managing the way you respond to what is happening to them.

12. Acknowledgment:

Don't worry about the stuff you don't have control over. Recognize that the one thing you can always control is your response and attitude, and make effective use of those attributes.

13. Endurance against failure:

View failure as an opportunity for growth and improvement, not a motive to give up. Be willing to continue the effort until you get it right.

14. Inevitable Positivity:

Stay positive also— especially— when you come across negative people. Elevate them; never get down to yourself. Don't let naysayers ruin your spirit of what you accomplish.

15. Congratulations:

Don't waste time envying the car, house, spouse, job, or family of anyone else. Instead, be thankful for what you have got. Instead of looking over your shoulder and being envious of what someone else has, focus on what you have achieved, and what you are going to achieve.

16. Too much tenacity:

It is just three words: Never give up.

17. Strong compass within:

When your sense of direction is internalized deeply, you will never have to worry about getting lost. Remain true to the course.

18.   Standards that are uncompromising:

Tough times or business problems are not good reasons for lowering the bar. Stick to your standards.

It takes practice and mindfulness to become a mentally strong person. To fix them involves tuning in to your bad habits and making a point of learning new habits. And sometimes it just means learning to get out of the way and letting things happen.

MENTAL TOUGHNESS IN EDUCATION

In education, mental toughness has emerged as a highly significant factor in youth development. The main challenges they encounter, and what they can do about them and how to deal with them, particularly as they encounter examinations or tests.

Mental toughness is a trait of personality which determines one's ability to consistently perform under stress and pressure. Mental toughness is a trait of personality which embraces ideas like attitude, character, resilience, and grit in a very practical way.

Research shows that mental toughness in education has been linked to a number of key factors, such as academic engagement, valuation of schoolwork, effective coping, thriving on pressure, achievement, well-being, behavior in the classroom, attendance, and change in transition.

Mental toughness combines resilience and trust or confidence;

- Resilience – the ability to bounce back from setbacks and failures.

- Trust – the ability to take advantage of situations and opportunities. The word "trust" as used in this area of study contains confidence inside of it. When you are confident, people will trust because courage defines the first quality of a warrior. When I was in high school, I was so confident up to a level that I do challenge my teachers, telling them I will teach them another method when I write my examinations. So they trust me!

This will allow you to "survive and thrive."

It is a state of mind and can be developed and improved as such in the same way as a physical condition. It has its roots in sport but has been recognized as a critically important feature in education, health and community services, and in the corporate sector over the past few years.

What are the benefits to individuals?

There are four key proven advantages to being mentally tough that relate to:

•   Performance – mentally hard people are delivering more, working more purposefully, showing more commitment to purpose, and being more competitive. This translates into better output, on-time delivery, and target delivery and better attendance. Mentally hard people achieve a performance uplift of 25 percent over others.

•   Behavior – people who are mentally tough are more positive, have a more "can do" attitude, respond positively to change and adversity, are more likely to contribute to a positive culture, take responsibility, and seek new responsibilities, opportunities, and activities.

•   Well-being – people who are mentally tough show better stress management, better attendance, are less likely to develop mental health problems, sleep better, and are less likely to bully. They are able to take stress in their step.

- Change – people who are psychologically strong usually have a can mentality and thus cope well in personal or organizational change and confusion situations.

What are the benefits of schools? The mentally tough teaching staff is more flexible, with a more positive culture and a higher level of performance. It is important for teachers to be mentally tough themselves to be able to create a mentally tough, high performance, and positive culture within their classrooms and students.

Mental toughness is a valuable ability in life that is gained through experience and observation of people's actions and feelings nearest to them. It is necessary to establish mental toughness within the teachers as key role models for students. Teachers have been shown to be able to have a causal effect on variables such as student absences and grade progression.

The benefit of implementing a Mental Toughness in Education program is that it provides a starting point and a clear and common framework and language for the process and the results. This fosters contemplation, dialogue, and openness about the attitude of a person towards mental toughness and, ideally, a commitment to change. To achieve a consistent increase in mental toughness and the associated benefits in modeling and improving mental toughness in students, this includes the use of appropriate training and seminars focused on techniques such as positive thinking, goal setting, attention management, or visualization to change habits and routines.

MENTAL TOUGHNESS IN SPORT

Mental toughness refers to a collection of psychological features central to optimum performance. Athletes, coaches, and sports psychologists have consistently implied mental toughness as one of the most important psychological features associated with sports success. Yet its conceptualization and measurement are nonconsensual. The purpose of this study is to review some of the emerging definitions and conceptualizations systematically and examine how mental toughness might be nurtured. This review considers both qualitative and quantitative approaches to mental toughness study with particular emphasis on models and the development of this Construct's measurement. While these discussions focus on the general aspects of mental toughness, we believe that many of the issues are relevant to scholars and practitioners who are interested in measuring psychological variables as they relate to sport, exercise, and other contexts for performance or achievement.

The success or failure of athletes is multifactorial. The combination of many factors, including physical, tactical, technical, and psychological factors, depends on that. The psychological factor is typically the determinant of a winner and a loser in sports. Mental ability contributed more than 50 percent to the success of athletes in competing against opponents. Furthermore, a study indicated that mental toughness was the most important for wrestling success (rated as 82 percent). They reported mental toughness in a study involving ten Olympians as one of the highest-ranked psychological features that determine the performance attained. However, the term mental toughness remains subjective despite its frequent use. In particular, it is often used to describe a broad term reflecting the ability of an athlete to cope effectively with training and competition requirements in an effort to remain resilient.

Mental toughness has consistently been referred to by athletes, coaches, and applied sports psychologists as one of the most important psychological characteristics related to results and success in elite sport. But it is probably one of the least understood terms used in sport psychology. A sport-specific use of this terminology is warranted to facilitate further understanding of this Construct.

A key question about mental toughness in sport is "is mental toughness an inheritance or developed?" Some studies revealed that it is inheritable, while some others debated that it is built based on key influencers of an individual's life (that is, parents, coaches, and environment).

Mental toughness could be inheritable if I am to acknowledge other researchers, but the minimal amount for offspring to build on. If you do not build on it, they have inherited nothing. But in my own opinion, mental toughness is built.

When I was a kid, I was not brilliant academically, whereas my father was so brilliant academically. When I eventually got into high school, I started building myself that I became so bright, intelligent, and smart, farther than my father. I do things my father cannot do. I think of impossible missions, in whom my father tells me to forget about that, but I still find a way to achieve them, and it amazes him. He always says, "You always think too big, wake up from your dream".

On the other hand, there are sharp and smart parents, and their children will be so dull. If he made a mistake once and did not get the expected result, he gives up and moves to another task. Why is he not like his parents? So I can say mental toughness is not inheritable. I stand with the argument that mental toughness is built. I became brilliant academically and intelligent the day I made up my mind that I will never give up no matter what. I repeat once again; mental toughness is built.

CHARACTERISTICS OF MENTAL TOUGHNESS

Mental toughness has been the subject of many years of discussion in sports literature. Indeed, due to the alignment and common framework that it carries, mental toughness has been related to both business and sporting worlds.

Ten key mental toughness characteristics among performers in the sport are enumerated below:

1.   Ability to bounce back from defeat — Defeat will be experienced by sports performers e.g., The defeat suffered by champion performers like Michael Phelps, Novak Djokovic; a great tennis player, Lionel Messi; a great footballer with six Ballon d'Or awards, and Lewis Hamilton; Formula 1 great driver. Elite performers, however, have that innate ability to bounce back. The ability to bounce back is imperative for restoring Positivity and confidence in oneself. In order to achieve future success, performers channel their deep inner sanctums and respond by fueling their fire on defeat. To put it another way, defeat hurts enough to bounce back.

2.   Resilience – A resilient performer will look at each task and perform to its maximum to achieve the ultimate objective. Resilience is related to the ability

to bounce back and to work under pressure to cope with it. Resilience is a characteristic that performers can use when using mental skills to build self-confidence. Tennis is a good example of resilience, where performers fight back from 2 sets during tournaments.

3. Consistent – Within their performance and training, performers must have consistency and stability. The drive theory is associated with forming habits, and the better you should become, the more you do something (e.g., a free throw in basketball). Consistency within your sport is also about mental and physical preparation.

4. Composed – Sport contains an array of emotions with which the outcomes can influence and impact. Composure purpose allows the performer to perform tasks with the maximum application and minimal energy expenditure. For example, the mind and body require balance before a successful execution of a gymnastic routine. Performers who fail may indeed be anxious about the result that leads to failure. Created nervousness and tension will only be subject to tightening of the body and confusing mind.

5. Motivation – There is no doubt that performers need intrinsic as well as extrinsic motivation to be champion athletes. The inner self-belief that outlines desire and commitment is imperative. Performers based on this inner self-belief

can use extrinsic motivation to influence their choices. The key to motivation has the ability to set and effectively achieve process-related goals.

6. Confidence – It is important to consider trust given the nature of sport and its fluctuating fortunes. There are a variety of models that direct the purpose of faith. In short, the ability to be aware that you can achieve a set goal or execute a particular skill can be related to confidence. When there is self-doubt, confidence levels will be low. When a performer builds confidence, levels of self-efficacy heighten.

7. Desire - The desire and willingness to achieve are closely aligned with confidence. Also, desire is formed from an inner conviction that it can achieve success. When teams have set goals and believe they can reach them, the assessment of positive body language is noticeable. Conversely, the opposite effect of poor body language occurs when teams are disjointed.

8. Organized - There will always be a top performer organized to achieve their goals. The organization is based on many aspects that are subtle but equally important to some. Preparation and punctual arrival are essential characteristics of the organization. It is also vital to follow critical instructions and understand these. For instance, an organized performer will most likely be prepared and focused on the task at hand.

9. Attention to detail – This is a crucial ingredient possessed by top performers. Within elite sport (performers or coaches), it is evident that something can be tactically spotted much faster than others. Considering that elite sport has fine margins within it, and then attention to detail becomes crucial. Indeed, there is evidence within some team sports of using GPS systems to assess how many ground performers covered it.

10. Determined - It is necessary to determine the performers who want to achieve success. Determination is formed from the self-belief within. It is by a determination that the performers become successful and find ways to advance to the next level. Recent examples of determined performers who have moved to the next level successfully include Andy Murray, England Rugby Union, and the Indian Test Team.

It is reflective practice, built into mental toughness. In order to be mentally tough, reflective practice should be used that offers opportunities to evaluate strengths and develop areas for improvement. One common strategy for aligning this opportunity is by setting targets. Taken together, mental toughness, reflective practice, and mental competencies are aligned to support performance and facilitate it.

SELF DISCIPLINE AND MENTAL TOUGHNESS

Mental toughness marks the start of every successful case. It all starts with the way you think. Mental tenacity is a prerequisite for self-discipline. This explains the difference between mental toughness and self-discipline as shown below from Economics in high school where we have "What to produce, how to produce, and when to produce"

Mental toughness— what to produce,

Self-discipline— how to create.

Self-discipline is one of the most significant and useful skills that everybody should have. This skill is essential in every area of life, and although most people recognize its importance, very few do anything to reinforce it.

Contrary to common belief, self-discipline does not mean being tough on yourself or living a restrictive, limited lifestyle. Self-discipline means self-control, which is a sign of your inner strength and self-control, actions, and reactions.

Self-discipline gives you the ability to stick to and follow your decisions, without changing your mind, and is, therefore, one of the most important requirements to achieve goals.

Possession of this skill allows you to persevere with your decisions and plans until you get them done. It also manifests as an inner strength that helps you to overcome addictions, procrastination, and laziness, and to carry on with whatever you do.

One of its main features is the ability to refuse instant gratification and pleasure in favor of some more significant gain, which requires time and effort to get it.

Self-discipline is one of the critical ingredients for success. It's expressed in various ways:

- Perseverance.

- Not giving up, despite failures and setbacks. It is self-control.

- Fitness to withstand distractions or temptations.

- Try again and again until you do what you're setting out to do.

Life puts challenges and problems on the path to success and achievement, and you have to act with perseverance and persistence in order to rise above them, and this, of course, requires self-discipline.

Possession of this ability leads to self-confidence and self-esteem, and consequently to happiness and contentment.

In contrast, lack of self-discipline leads to problems of failure, loss, health and relationships, obesity, and other problems.

Also useful is this skill to overcome eating disorders, addictions, smoking, drinking, and negative habits. You also need it to get you sitting and studying, Exercise your body, develop new skills, and spiritual growth and meditation for self-improvement.

As mentioned earlier, most people recognize the importance and benefits of self-discipline, but very few take real steps to develop and strengthen self-discipline.

Like any other skill, you can, however, reinforce this ability. This is done through training and exercises.

<u>Benefits from self-discipline and importance Self-discipline helps:</u>

- Do not act rashly or on impulses.

- Complete your promises to yourself and to others.

- Surmounting laziness and procrastination.

- Continue to work on a project, even after the initial rush of excitement has faded away.

- Go to the gym, go walking or swimming, also if your mind tells you to stay home and watch television.

- Continue to work on your diet and withstand the temptation to eat fattening food.

- Arise early in the morning.

- Get over the habit of watching too much television.

- Read a book, and read it to the last page.

- Think regularly.

Strengthening your self-discipline will be easier for you if you:

1. Understand the importance of that in your life.

2. Make yourself aware of your undisciplined conduct and its consequences. When this awareness increases, you'll be more convinced of the need to make a life change.

3. Make an effort to act and act according to your decisions, regardless of laziness, the tendency to procrastinate, or the desire to give up and stop what you're doing.

4. Even though it is currently weak, you can strengthen your self-disciple with the help of special simple exercises that you can practice at any time or place.

<u>How to develop self-discipline</u>

The greatest struggle is always within ourselves, like everything else that brings progress. Therefore you have to learn self-discipline.

When you are facing a hot-fudge sundae or the prospect of sleeping in versus hitting the gym, it may be hard to believe, but studies show that people with self-discipline are happier.

People with a higher degree of self-control spend less time debating whether to indulge in behaviors that harm their health and are able to make more easily positive decisions. They are not letting their choices be dictated by impulses or feelings. Instead, they make decisions that are level-headed. As a consequence, they tend to feel more content with their lives.

There are things you can do to learn to discipline yourself and gain the will to live a happier life. If you want to take control of your habits and choices, here are the ten (10) most powerful things you can do to master self-discipline:

1.   Know your shortcomings.

We all have deficits. Whether it is snacks like potato chips or chocolate chip cookies, or technology like Facebook or the latest addictive game app, they do have similar effects on us.

Recognize your shortcomings no matter what they may be. Too often, people either try to pretend they don't have their vulnerabilities or cover up any pitfalls in their lives. Own up to your shortcomings. Until you do, you can't overcome these.

2.   Eliminate the temptations.

As the saying goes, "out of sight, out of mind." It may sound dumb, but this sentence offers powerful advice. You'll greatly enhance your self-discipline by simply removing your biggest temptations from your environment.

Do not buy junk food if you wish to eat healthier. Turn off notifications and silence your mobile phone if you want to improve your productivity at work. The fewer distractions you get, the more focused you will be on achieving your goals. Set yourself to success by dismantling bad influences.

3.   Set clear goals and have a plan for implementation.

If you hope to achieve self-discipline, you'll need to have a clear vision of what you're hoping to achieve. You also need to get an understanding of what you mean by success. After all, it's easy to lose your way or get sidetracked, if you don't know where you are going.

A clear plan outlines every step you need to take to reach your targets. The figure who you are and what you're up to. Create a mantra to keep a focus on yourself. Successful individuals use this technique to stay on track and set a clear finish line.

4. Build your discipline on yourself.

We are not born with self-discipline— it is an acquired behavior. And it requires daily practice and repetition, just like any other skill you wish to master. Just like going to the gym, it takes a lot of work for willpower and self-discipline. It can be draining the effort and focus which self-discipline requires.

As time goes by, keeping your willpower in check may become more and more difficult. The higher the temptation or decision, the more challenging it may feel to address other tasks that require self-control, too. Thus work by daily diligence on building your self-discipline.

5. By keeping it simple, they create new habits.

At first, acquiring self-discipline and working to inculcate a new habit can feel daunting, especially if you focus on the whole task at hand. Just keep it simple to avoid feeling intimidated. Bridge your goal into small, practical steps. Instead of trying to change everything at once, focus on consistently doing one thing and master self-discipline with that objective in mind.

If you're trying to get into shape, start with 10 or 15 minutes of work out a day. If you're trying to achieve better sleeping habits, begin by going to bed every night 15 minutes before. If you want to eat healthier, start with lunch the evening before you take it with you in the morning. Take steps for baby. Eventually, you can add more targets to your list when you're ready.

6. Eat often, and eat well.

The feeling of being angry— that angry, annoyed, irritated feeling you get when you're hungry — is real and can have a significant impact on your willpower. Research has shown that low sugar in the blood often weakens a person's resolve and makes you grumpy and pessimistic.

Your ability to concentrate suffers when you're hungry, and your brain doesn't work as well. Your self-control in all areas, including diet, exercise, work, and relationships, is likely weakened. So you fuel up with healthy snacks and regular meals to stay in control.

7. Change your perception of the power of will.

What you think is what you are, and what you attract is what you are for. What you are drawing is what is going to happen in your life. You have enough power and authority to bring to pass what you want to see happening in your life. You can achieve that if you can think of it. Be careful, it matters a lot what you think, and determines the outcome of your life.

When you know you have a small amount of willpower, you're not possibly going to exceed those limits. If you don't put a limit on your self-control, you're less likely to exhaust yourself before you meet your objectives.

In short, our inner conceptions about willpower and self-control may determine how much we have of them. If you can remove these mental obstacles and truly believe you can, then you will be giving yourself an extra boost of motivation to make those goals a reality.

8.   Donate a backup plan for yourself.

Psychologists use a technique called "implementation intention" to boost willpower. That's when you give yourself a plan to deal with a potentially challenging situation that you know will likely face. Imagine, for example, that you're working on healthier eating, but you're on your way to a party where food is being served.

Before you go, tell yourself that you will be sipping a glass of water instead of diving into a plate of cheese and crackers, and focus on mixing. Going in with a plan will help give you the mindset and the necessary self-control for the situation. You'll also save energy by not having to make a sudden emotional decision.

9.   Praise yourself.

Give yourself something to be excited about when you plan a reward to accomplish your goals. Just like when you were a little kid, having something to look forward to gives you the motivation to be successful.

Anticipation is strong. This gives you something to reflect and concentrate on so that you don't just worry about what you're trying to change. And when you attain your goal, you will find a new purpose and a unique reward to keep moving forward.

10.   Forgive yourself and go ahead.

We still fall short, even with all of our best intentions and well-laid plans. It does happen. You're going to have ups and downs, big successes, and dismal failures. The key is to stay on the move.

If you are stumbling, then recognize what caused it and move on. Don't let yourself be wrapped up in guilt, anger, or frustration, for these emotions will only drag you further down and hamper future progress. Learn from your mistakes and forgive. Then get your head back into the game and concentrate on your goals.

Why we don't have self-discipline, and how we can tackle it or start it

One of the most crucial life skills to develop is the ability to self-discipline for those just starting in life (and everyone else!).

It is like a superpower: I started to exercise and eat healthier and meditate and write more when I developed some self-discipline, I quit eating junk and started eating good foods, I started making predictions and wrote books, I read more and work earlier. I'm not perfect, but I've learned a lot.

But if you don't develop self-discipline, it causes problems: problems with your health, distraction, procrastination, financial problems, clutter, things that pile up and overwhelm you, and much more.

Developing so is such an important skill, but most people don't know where to begin. This book is also written to help get you started.

1. Finding Motivation:

How do you even get motivated to start? Most of us don't want to ponder our lack of discipline, let alone take a bunch of actions. The motivation for me came from realizing that what I did wasn't working. Ignoring the issues only made matters worse. Trying to be careful but doing it half-assuredly only made me feel bad about myself. To be absolutely undisciplined has caused a lot of pain to me.

We can start to practice with motivations— or whatever motivations move you the most.

2.   Small Actions:

Taking small actions is one of the most important things you can do to get better at self-discipline. Tackling huge, bullying projects can seem overwhelming, so don't. Instead, tackle simple actions, stuff so small that you can't say no. When I started pushups early in the morning, for example, it was when I was in my first year in a tertiary institution that my friends used to laugh at me because of my lean body form. So I made up my mind to stay with twenty pushups each morning when I wake up. I can go over forty pushups today and as many as fifty if I like it.

3.   Discomfort Training:

One of the reasons we're not self-disciplined is that we're hiding from the rough, uncomfortable things. We'd rather do the familiar, comfortable, easy stuff. And we crash into distractions, photos, games instead of facing up to our challenging, stressful tasks or finances. This running out of discomfort has ruined our lives. What you can say to yourself is you are running done. You will step into discomfort, a little at a time, and you will get good at being uncomfortable. This is one more superpower of yours.

When I started pushing in a tertiary institution, I used to flip off when I started feeling the discomfort until I was told by a sports official in my institution, "When you start feeling pain, then you start doing the real and effective pushes." Then I stopped flipping off and focused more on a certain number of pushups to do.

Push yourself into discomfort, one small task at a time. See how it feels. See, it is not the end of the world. See that you're genius enough to handle discomfort, and the results are worth it.

4. Mindfulness and Urges:

You're going to have the desire to stop or put off something for now. Those urges are not serving you well. Instead, develop awareness around these urges, and see that you need not follow them.

A good way to do that is to give yourself a time where you can only do X. For starters, you can do nothing for the next 10 minutes but write your book chapter (or exercise, meditate, etc.). You will see it easily when you have the urge to procrastinate or run into distractions because you either write the book or you are not. You have to either write your book chapter or sit there and do nothing, when you have the urge, tell yourself you can't follow it.

5. Interval Training:

You can train yourself using interval training if you combine the above items into a burst system or intervals:

- Set your intention to practice self-discipline and not hurt yourself anymore.

- Focus on the task (writing, drawing, strength training, meditation, etc.);

- Set a 10-minute timer. If 10 is too long, then five minutes is beautiful too. Don't go any longer until at 10 minutes you get right, then increase to 12 and eventually 15. I don't find that I need to go beyond 15-20 minutes, even when I kick my ass.

- Do nothing but sit there and watch your urges, or push through the task to your discomfort.

- Give yourself a 5minute break when the timer goes off.

- Repeat.

You should prepare for several times, or maybe an hour or two. Then take a longer break, and afterward do another set of intervals.

This kind of interval training is fantastic because it's not that hard, you're really training yourself in discomfort and watching urges, and that way you can get a lot done. This is the tenet behind the successes of Lionel Messi and Cristiano Ronaldo. These two soccer players train more than any other player in the world, and it has exuberantly helped them achieve.

Some good examples of Self-discipline

Some good examples of self-discipline must start from within if your entire thinking process is to be filtered. Here are just a few examples of good discipline.

1.   Wake up early: It rejuvenates your mind and monitors your thinking process all day long. Someone like me wakes up every day at 5 a.m., even if I have no place to go or nothing to do. He was part of me.

2.   Respect your parents: These are priceless things they do for you. Show your devotion to them by word or deed. Let it be to praise your mom on her food, or to thank your dad for dropping you in the place of your friend.

3.   Reduce feelings like jealousy and hate; they reduce your effectiveness.

4. Respect for others: Respect must be shown to all. As always said, respect is mutual. You never undermine or underestimate anybody because tomorrow, anyone can be great.

5. Enjoy life to the full: Yes, enjoying reading it right doesn't mean leaving fun behind.

6. Love yourself and value yourself.

RESILIENT LEADERSHIP

Resilient leadership in all four Cs requires mental toughness, namely discipline, dedication, challenge, and trust.

Control– Control means a sense of self-worth and explains to what degree a person feels in control of his or her life and circumstances. Importantly it also describes how much they can regulate their emotions showing.

A psychologically hard person will generally just "go on with it" regardless of how they feel and how optimistic their approach can often lift the spirits of those around them.

Commitment— Commitment is about target orientation and 'stickability'. It explains to what degree somebody is prepared to set goals on what they need to do and make tangible commitments that they will work hard to deliver on once they have made them.

Taken together, discipline and determination are what most people mean when they speak of resilience, and in reality, they are a strong response to adversity. But resilience is primarily a passive attribute and is just one aspect of Mental Toughness.

Challenge— Challenge explains how far the person pushes back its limits, embraces change, and accepts the risk. It's all about getting all the outcomes - positive and adverse.

Mentally hard people see difficulties, transition, and hardship as opportunities rather than risks, and they will appreciate the opportunity to learn and grow in a new situation that has been unknown. Someone whose score is high on difficulty will typically enjoy new places, new people, innovation, and creativity.

Confidence– Confidence completes the picture and defines an individual's self-belief in his or her ability and the interpersonal confidence he or she has to control others and deal with conflict and challenge. Mentally hard people scoring high in confidence when faced with a challenge will have the self-confidence to handle the situation, and the inner strength to stand their ground when necessary. Their trust helps them to express their views and be confident in addressing challenges boldly.

Every one of these 4 C's has a significant effect on your mental toughness.

Organizations require leadership, which is resilient. They also need to be able to perform under extreme pressure at the highest level with the continuous and growing demand for leaders to enhance organizational performance. They need to be mentally tough enough to make rational and correct decisions and to help the people around them to do this.

You need to be mentally tough to be an active and successful leaders. They need to set and communicate the vision, bring people with them on the road, strive for success, and seize opportunities from the inevitable setbacks and failures along the way. Such roles require effective leadership, and mental toughness requires effective leadership.

A leader's job is to encourage, influence, and direct people's success towards the goals desired. Being a successful and resilient leader helps you attain this through more significant commitment. This commitment is critical, and indeed the high quality of the leadership capacity measures identifies engagement as two of the three core leadership skills:

- Individual engagement

- Team engagement

- Determination to deliver.

For many people in leadership positions, both work and life are becoming more difficult, and many now report increasing stress on them. Mental Toughness is a significant factor in determining how a person responds to stress, pressure, and challenge—and how that impacts efficiency, health, and positive behaviors.

Mental toughness offers growth tools for leaders and plans to help them perform under pressure and encourage others around them. This leads to better efficiency, health, and an improved work-life balance in many instances.

Mental Toughness Partners run "Mental Toughness Development Programs for Leaders" to help them develop techniques for under-pressure success, leading to better performance, well-being, and better work-life balance. Tell us to learn more about robust leadership development and coaching packages.

BUILDING A RESILIENT ORGANIZATION

Building a resilient organization is vital to the success of all companies in these ever-changing times. Mental Toughness Partners run specific programs on "Building Resilient Organizations" to assist the company in cultivating an attitude of organizational toughness, improving its employees ' mental toughness, and creating a positive atmosphere and enhancing well-being. This, in turn, will lead to performance enhancement.

Mental toughness will provide you with the tools and resources to execute in-house programs. Organizations face rapid structural change through economic uncertainty and technological advancement, which threatens their survival unless they can react swiftly and decisively to it. Hence it is vital to develop robust organizations.

In these situations, one of the fundamental keys to success is their workers ' endurance and mental toughness. They will adapt their attitude through specialized resilience training to perceive difficulty and change as an opportunity, not a danger, which in turn creates a better culture and increases retention and productivity.

Resilient workers are essential to productive enterprises. After all, it is the people who are the lifeblood of any organization, whether times are good or bad. When hiring or promoting employees, endurance, and mental stability is not at the top of the checklist for decision making. But maybe they should. Mental toughness can improve the performance of a person by up to 25 percent, so consider the impact on the overall business if the mental toughness of everybody can be improved!

In some other particular areas of life, I'll like to think about mental toughness. These are areas in which we face comprehensive challenges and which in effect involve mental toughness that includes;

- BUSINESS- everybody is a businessman or businesswoman either we like or not because we buy and sell. Either you are employed or not. At the point you are getting an employment appointment, you would negotiate your remuneration. In other words, it is a form of business.

- MILITARY

- POLITICS- one of the areas of life where we encounter a tough mental challenge is politics. The stress, tension, and pressure that come with aspiration, campaign, and election most especially cannot be accounted for nor evaluated.

Let us talk about them extensively, one after the other below.

MENTAL TOUGHNESS

IN BUSINESS

How many days are you feeling tired and confused all day? Would you fall into the trap of jumping from one mission to another without finishing the actual project? Were you overwhelmed with feelings of disorganization, lack of direction, and vagueness of thought? Practicing mental toughness in all that you do is an important factor in good results.

Mental toughness is an attribute that colors how you will accomplish a mission and how effectively you can adapt to your environment and its challenges. This book shows how mental toughness is a critical factor that helps you to perform to the best of your ability. It's a quality that can be improved or strengthened in several ways; it will increase your awareness. It is a quality that can be developed or enhanced in many ways; it will increase your knowledge of your mental toughness and show you how you can achieve business success when you apply this.

What is mental toughness?

Although there are many definitions of mental toughness, also known as mental strength, the ability to recover from setbacks and disappointments, is the standard and generally accepted concept from the fields of sport and business, to be mentally resilient, to have a healthy self-confidence, to persevere in the challenges and to respond effectively to situations with calmness, concentration, and presence of mind.

This mastered ability is quickly becoming a competitive edge for athletes, business professionals, and today in life as a whole. Mental toughness is a strength in life, a trait, and a mentality that lets you succeed in business and life. It takes you through the rough times and empowers you with less effort, less pressure, and less tension to do your best. You will become a more robust and positive person in whatever you do, once you have learned and developed this mindset within yourself.

My experience working with business professionals like my Father, my father's friend, my lecturers, shows that mental toughness is the fundamental character trait that drives individual performance and helps other mental abilities, such as courage, stamina, and mental flexibility to perform at their best.

CHANGE THE MENTAL HABITS

Lydia, a new leader in a telecommunications company, was asked by her manager to present at a conference for the company. She's talked to smaller audiences before, but that would be her first encounter with a massive crowd of a thousand. She experiences the pressure to perform well. For her, it would be easy to make up some reason and go back out.

She embraces the challenge. She avoids relying on anxiety to be mentally tough and fills her mind with pessimistic what-ifs. Instead, she prepares her presentation and herself in the eye of her mind by re-experiencing those peak performance moments when she successfully presented them.

She imagines incorporating them in her latest presentation as she feels the tension in these moments. She understands that she has to deal with her past habits to help her develop new ones and be mentally tough. She understands that if she imagines vividly having a new pattern, her brain will automatically begin to rewire for the mental connection to be made.

Lydia is gaining mental toughness, and she will be ready to present. A word of caution: Mental toughness doesn't mean you're becoming a bully, or you're feeling the need to show unruly or arrogant behaviors towards someone or something to show your mental power.

What this means is that you have learned and built your inner strength, determination, versatility, and focused fortification to such an extent that you can manage whatever comes your way, surpass your ordinary expectations and be optimally efficient and successful in life. Seen from a perspective of martial arts, it is a defensive art of self-management rather than an aggressive one.

With Mental Toughness, People in business — whether people in business or employees — you will achieve success are inspired to succeed in several ways. Whether you're leading a company and team (e.g., running a mutual fund, coordinating a business development, strategizing) or engaging individually as a salesperson or successful developer, the success outlook becomes more apparent when you exercise mental toughness in all you do.

Some of the benefits you gain from mental toughness are your ability to

- have a clear vision, direction, and plan that contribute to personal and professional objectives being achieved;

- refocus your thoughts as the situation changes;

- outperform your rivals by being continuously concentrated, optimistic, and under pressure;

- perform to your best to be positive;

Your superiority in competition starts first in your mind.

Success in business and life depends on your capacity not only to learn what you do but also what you think and how you feel. This means that human action starts in the mind— joining emotions, desired results, imagination, and ingenuity.

Feeling regulated is the first step towards being in control. You should grow your mind in order to enhance your results and the competitive advantage. To become a business and life champion, you need to be a winner in your head first. Think of a time when something like this happened to you, as you read through the story below.

Michael is a well-liked and highly respected sales professional. He is relaxed, concentrated, and in charge when making presentations to prospects. Michael reaches the buyer's office on this particular sales call and confidently offers his name to the receptionist. There are seven candidates expected to present, including himself, all competing for one deal. As Michael looks around, he sees many of them rehearsing quietly; others look uncomfortable.

Michael realizes that it is too late to prepare and to rehearse when the presentation is only a few minutes away. He is confident and prepared. He's done hundreds of mock presentations in his mind, and it's becoming a routine that demonstrates confidence. Previously, he rehearsed, exercised, and visualized his desired results so that he could resolve every question and answer every challenge. He knows that managing questions means controlling the presentation's speed, direction, and sales.

The receptionist calls a name for Michael. He steps into the private office with faith; confident he can beat his rivals and win the deal. He's in the moment, mentally and emotionally. His thoughts centered on this presentation alone, not on the last or the next. He fills his mind with an attitude of can-do and projects his desired result. He is playing to win.

CONCLUSION

Thank you for reading all this book!

Remember when you sat at square one, unable to release yourself from the overthinking chains? I know that well— I was there myself. To stand up and say, I'm ready to make a change, takes a lot of courage. It makes me sad to think that, in their whole lives, many individuals continue to overthink and over-analyze, and ignoring the insights and understanding a free mind can understand. It's easy to slip into the stress-free routines of mindless eating, searching every few minutes for a phone or tablet, and going to bed very late until the body is out of order. Often, giving in seems too easy, and letting what is easy overshadows what it is worth working for. You don't need to be a slave to overthinking, and maybe you can take what you've experienced to help change the lives of people around you.

Perhaps you know someone who seems to tend to overthink, endure daily problems and worry just like you were at the beginning of your journey. Talk about reaching out and sharing what you have found. Nothing feels better than sharing new experiences with someone who can use them to make the positive changes in themselves that you have seen happen. Maybe he's a boss, a partner, or a close friend. Many individuals from different walks of life would benefit from this book's life-changing guides, so why not share your story!

You have already taken a step towards your improvement.
Best wishes!

www.ingramcontent.com/pod-product-compliance
Lightning Source LLC
Chambersburg PA
CBHW062140100526
44589CB00014B/1636